STRESS MANAGEMENT
THROUGH SPIRITUALITY

Stress Management through Spirituality

Dhyāna Ratna S.K. Rajan

MOTILAL BANARSIDASS
INTERNATIONAL
DELHI

First Edition : Delhi, 2026

ISBN : 978-93-47683-49-7

Also available at
MOTILAL BANARSIDASS INTERNATIONAL
H.O. : 41 U.A. Bungalow Road, (Back Lane) Jawahar Nagar, Delhi - 110 007
4261 (Basement) Lane #3, Ansari Road, Darya Ganj, New Delhi - 110 002
203 Royapettah High Road, Mylapore, Chennai - 600 004
12/1A, 2nd Floor, Bankim Chatterjee Street, Kolkata - 700 073
Stockist : Motilal Books, Ashok Rajpath, Near Kali Mandir, Patna - 800 004

Printed in India
MOTILAL BANARSIDASS INTERNATIONAL

Preface

Stress has emerged as one of the most pervasive challenges of contemporary life, silently influencing physical health, emotional well-being, and mental clarity. While stress is a natural response that equips the human system to meet life's demands, its persistent and unmanaged expression has become a major contributor to modern ailments and inner unrest.

The pressures of professional performance, academic competition, economic uncertainty, environmental challenges, and rapid social change have placed unprecedented demands on individuals across all age groups. What is often overlooked is that stress is shaped not merely by external circumstances, but by the way the mind interprets and responds to them. This understanding forms the foundation of both medical science and spiritual wisdom.

Chronic stress weakens resilience, impairs judgment, and disrupts the delicate balance between body and mind. Its effects are now visible even among children and adolescents, underscoring the need for early awareness, emotional nurturing, and compassionate guidance.

This booklet serves as a timely and thoughtful guide, offering clarity on the nature of stress and practical insights for managing it effectively. By integrating awareness, self-regulation, and inner balance, it reminds us that true well-being arises when the mind is anchored in calmness. In such inner steadiness, health is preserved, purpose is strengthened, and life is lived with greater harmony

The book emphasises the role of the balance to be maintained between body, mind and the intellect to assist soulfull living, so that it becomes possible to smooth away stresses with ease. Meditation and yoga are recommended as they are conscious and systematic processes for the complete physical, mental, intellectual, emotional and spiritual development of any human being. Though life's challenges cannot always be controlled, our responses can be strengthened. Developing effective coping skills enables individuals to regain equilibrium, enhance well-being, and transform stress from a destructive force into an opportunity for growth and inner strength.

Dhyāna Ratna S.K. Rajan
Founder Chairman
Soulfull Federation Trust® &
Chairman,
International Federation of Spiritual Scientists

Foreword

What is increasingly threatening the individual and the world is the new pandemic — depression, stress, anxiety. Nothing can stop the man with the right mental attitude from achieving his goal; nothing on earth can help the man with the wrong mental attitude. Death is not the greatest loss in life. The greatest loss is what dies inside us while we live.

The mind is in its own place, and in itself can make a heaven of hell, a hell of heaven. Happiness depends upon ourselves. We make our own hell or heaven by our thoughts, words and deeds.In an era marked by relentless pace, rising expectations, and growing uncertainties, stress has emerged as a silent yet pervasive threat to human well-being. Its impact spans across age groups, professions, and social strata, affecting physical health, emotional balance, and mental clarity. The alarming rise in stress-related disorders and student distress in India underscores the urgent need for awareness and effective coping strategies. Stress Management is neither a punishment nor a surgery — but a life skill — essential for physical health, mental clarity, meaningful relationships, and sustained success.

This timely book — STRESS MANAGEMENT THROUGH SPIRITUALITY, authored by Dhyāna Ratna S. K. Rajan, offers readers a clear, practical, and compassionate guide to understanding stress and managing it constructively. Drawing upon experience, insight, and sensitivity to contemporary challenges, the author presents actionable methods to cultivate   resilience and inner balance.

The inclusion of a dedicated chapter for parents and children further enhances the relevance of this work. Meditation, Yoga is the surest way of managing stress, depression and anxiety of the individual, the family, the society and the nation, to effectively manage all difficult stressful situations and to create a world without war and where there is harmony, justice, peace, prosperity and fairplay for everyone.

This book will certainly serve as a valuable resource for individuals, families, educators, and professionals seeking a stress- free, healthier, more peaceful and harmonious life for everyone.

D R Kaarthikeyan, IPS (R)
Padma Shri Awardee,
Former Director CBI, DG CRPF, NHRC
Chief Adviser, International Federation
of Spiritual Scientists

Introduction

Stress is an inseparable part of human life, yet it is often misunderstood and poorly managed. In its essence, stress is a natural biological and psychological response that prepares an individual to meet life's demands. When balanced, this response enhances alertness, efficiency, and personal growth. However, when pressure becomes continuous and unresolved, stress turns into distress—gradually eroding physical health, emotional stability, and mental clarity.

The modern era has amplified stressors manifold. Competitive workplaces, academic pressures, economic uncertainty, environmental degradation, digital overload, and strained interpersonal relationships have made daily life increasingly demanding. Crucially, stress does not arise merely from events themselves, but from the way individuals perceive and respond to them. While some adapt with composure, others experience anxiety, frustration, and exhaustion, thereby intensifying their burden.

The impact of unmanaged stress is evident across society—declining well-being, reduced productivity, lifestyle disorders, and emotional alienation. Alarmingly, even children and students are no longer spared, highlighting the urgent need for compassionate nurturing and emotional resilience.

While life's circumstances may not always be altered, one's inner response can be refined. A calm mind, cultivated through awareness, balance, and right understanding, restores harmony within. When inner stillness guides action, stress loses its grip and life regains meaning, purpose, and quiet strength.

Contents

Section B

Section A

Concept of Stress

Definition and Meanings

Latin Word – Strictus

French Word – Estrece

Meaning: "To Draw Tight"

Dictionary Meaning: Pressure, Hardship, Force, Strain, Tension

World Health Organisation—Definition Of Health

"Health Is A Complete State Of Physical,Mental And Social Well-Being And Not Merely The Absence Of Disease."

STRESS—Indian Thought

Origin of the word: "*KLESHA*" (in Sanskrit) is in the root "*KHIS* "--- which means "torment", "cause pain " or "to afflict ."

These are a set of "Hindering Factors" on the Mental Process which act as "Restrictions" or "Hinderances. "

STRESS—Definitions

- "A condition arising from the interaction of people and their jobs,characterised by changes within the people that force them to deviate from their normal functioning. "

- Stress is also defined as "an adaptive response to an external situation that results in physical ,psychological and/or behavioural deviations for organisational participants."

What is Stress?
(Psychological Point of View)

A. Pressure or demand on the system when available resources are not adequate to cope with.

B. It is a transaction between the person and the environment in which the situation is viewed by the individual as in some way exceeding the person's resources to cope and endangering his/her well-being.

Operation of Stress

Levels at Which Stress Operates

Physical Stress

- Arises from conditions such as:
  - Accidents
  - Burns
  - Major surgeries
  - Severe infections

- These place direct demands on the entire physiology.

- Modern life has sharply increased physical trauma, with accidents becoming a major cause of mortality.

Psychological / Emotional Stress

- May occur independently or as a reaction to physical stress.

- Common triggers include:
  - Fear, anxiety, tension, worry
  - Anger, jealousy, hatred
  - Emotional conflicts and excitement

- Can be:

  — Acute, requiring immediate adaptation

  — Chronic, leaving deep subconscious impressions and prolonged inner tension

Stress in Modern Society

- Rapid industrialization, high-speed living, and constant stimulation expose individuals to continuous stressors.

- Modern man:

  — Thinks and acts faster than earlier generations

  — Often exceeds optimal limits of mental and physical efficiency

  — Becomes emotionally hypersensitive, reacting intensely to trivial issues

- Social consequences include:

  — Relationship breakdowns

  — Rising divorce rates

  — Emotional instability and impulsive behavior

Suppression and its Consequences

- Suppressing emotional stress through:

  — Drugs

  — Substances

  — Emotional repression

- Leads to:

  — Numbing of the nervous system

  — Accumulation of unresolved emotional energy

  — Increased vulnerability to stress-related illnesses

Stress Reaction – A Common Outcome

- Regardless of whether stress is physical, psychological, or emotional, the body responds with a specific and predictable physiological pattern.

- This consistent pattern of bodily changes is known as the Stress Reaction.

Stress—Causes & Indications

Indications of Stress

- Sleep Disturbance
- High Blood Pressure
- Loss of Appetite
- Indigestion
- Inexplicable Muscle Pain/ Fatigue
- Low Productivity

Causes of Torment or Stress

Faulty evaluation of one or more of the following :

- Self-Appraisal
- Object Appraisal
- Threat Appraisal
- Coping Orientation

Group Stressors

- Interpersonal conflict
- Expectations from the group
- Low morale

- Low cohesiveness
- Lack of Free Flow of Communication

Organisational Stress

- Occupational demands
- Conflict
- Interpersonal Relations
- Work overload/underload
- Role conflict, ambiguity

Extra-Organisational Stress

- Family life events
- Social/Technological changes
- Economic/financial aspects
- Relocation
- "On the move" lifestyle

Types of Stressors

A. Personal

- Physiological
- Psychological

B. Situational — Interpersonal transactions, conflict, aggression, etc.

C. Environmental — Natural calamities, extreme temperature, work/family/residence

Stress Reaction – A Common Outcome

Regardless of whether stress is physical, psychological, or emotional, the body responds with a specific and predictable physiological pattern.

This consistent pattern of bodily changes is known as the Stress Reaction.

Stress and Its Measurement

Because the experience of stress is so complex and varies from one person to another, even in the same circumstances,stress is difficult to measure.

Stress Varies Individually

- Even in the same circumstances, people experience stress differently.

- This makes stress difficult to measure objectively.

Early Approaches to Measuring Stress

- Researchers designed instruments to measure stress through life events.

- Negative events (loss of a job, death of a loved one) are highly stressful.

- **Positive events** (starting college, getting married) can also be stressful.

- The key factor: **total impact of life changes** and **readjustment is required**.

Health Effects of Life Event Stress

- Studies show strong links between life changes and illnesses.

- Stress has been related to:
    - Sudden cardiac death
    - Diabetes
    - Complications in pregnancy and birth
    - Chronic illnesses
    - Multiple sclerosis
    - Minor physical problems

Shift to Everyday Stressors (Daily Hassles and Uplifts)

- Researchers now focus on **daily hassles** (e.g., owing money) and **daily uplifts** (e.g., staying fit).

- Some experts argue that **daily hassles** may affect health and mood more than major life events.

Common daily hassles by group

- **College students:** anxiety about wasting time, meeting high standards, loneliness.

- **Middle-aged people:** worries about health and money.

- **Professionals:** too much work, not enough time, difficulty relaxing.

- **All groups:** misplacing things, concerns about physical appearance, having too many tasks.

Impact of daily hassles on health

- Frequent, intense hassles are strongly linked to **poor psychological and physical health**.

Personal and Situational Factors in Stress

Our overall experience of stress is shaped by both personal and situational factors. Some of the most common ones are explained below:

Personal Factors

- **Perception of stress:** How we interpret a stressful event can make it feel more or less overwhelming. For example, some people see criticism of their work as a personal attack, becoming upset and wasting energy, defending themselves. Others view the same criticism as a challenge to improve, which reduces stress.

- **Personality traits:** People with inner doubts, low self-esteem, or suspicious tendencies may find even routine daily demands stressful.

- **Type A personality:** Those with Type A traits—highly competitive, impatient, and driven by strict standards—often live under constant pressure. They talk, walk, and eat quickly, and pride themselves on finishing tasks faster than others.

This relentless pace keeps them under stress and makes them more prone to heart disease.

Situational Factors

- **Life changes:** Stress often comes from the combined effect of multiple challenges. For instance, dealing with car troubles, a sick family member, and workplace crises, at the same time is far more stressful than facing any one of these alone.

- **Unpredictable events:** Sudden incidents, such as automobile accidents, are highly stressful. The threat of physical harm—like kidnapping or combat situations—intensifies stress dramatically.

- **High-alert jobs:** Certain professions, such as air traffic controllers, astronauts, or nuclear reactor workers, require constant vigilance. This ongoing alertness is a growing source of stress.

- **Lack of control:** Feeling powerless in a stressful situation worsens its impact. Studies show that workers in jobs with high demands but little control—like waiters or assembly-line staff—are five times more likely to develop coronary heart disease compared to those with greater autonomy.

Life Events that Trigger Stress in an Individual—Self-Evaluation of Life-Change Risk

Sr. No.	Event	Life Change Units
1.	Death of Spouse or Close One	100
2.	Divorce	75
3.	Death of a Close Family Member	50
4.	Personal Injury or Illness	53
5.	Loss of Job	50
6.	Retirement	45
7.	Change—Job/Working Conditions	40
8.	Financial Losses	45
9.	Change in Place of Work	35
10.	Change in Residence	30
11.	Addition in Family Due to Birth	39
12.	Pressure Due to Debts	38
13.	Employer's Demands	37
14.	Change in Sleeping Habits	20
15.	Change in Eating Habits	15
16.	Minor Violation of Law	13

The Stress Scale above indicates that each event is given a score that represents the amount of readjustment a person has to make in his or her won life as a result of a change. People with high life changing units have the highest risk.

If your Life-Change Units total 150-199, there is a mild chance of some illness in the coming year. If the total is 250-299 LCUs, you have a moderate risk. Over 300 points put you in the group very likely to suffer serious physical or emotional illness.

Managing Stress — General Principles

How to manage stress in any and every situation needs a complete understanding of our own capacities, our priorities, motivational levels etc. Developing proper and good human relations, positive self-esteem and capacity to harness the will, calm the mind and steady the emotions are all indispensable in coping with stress. Building resilience and adapting your response can make a significant difference. Managing stress means taking charge, directing and controlling our responses to stressors, thereby modifying the overall stress. There are many ways to accomplish this goal, but most of them fall under two major ways : a. modifying our environment and b. altering ourselves in some way that would tackle stress effectively.

Modifying Your Environment to Tackle Stress

A refrigerator that you had purchased has landed at your residence but you discover that the cooling effect is minimal and that that is not the model you wanted. What should you do ? You could tell the clerk in the showroom that there has beena mistake and then proceed to order and obtain the exact model you needed. Or else you could seek a refund and cancel the order, thereby making sure that you don't buy anything from that store anymore. Another option would be to refuse accepting that order and, instead, choose another refrigerator more to your liking and brand from among those already in stock.

These responses illustrate three basic ways to modify your environment : assertiveness, withdrawal, or compromise.

Let's examine these strategies :

Stress can often be reduced not by changing ourselves alone, but by changing how we respond to stressful situations. Three practical approaches are **Assertiveness, Withdrawal, and Compromise.**

1. Assertiveness – The Healthy First Choice

- Assertiveness means **clearly expressing your needs, feelings, and rights** without violating those of others.

- It directly addresses the **source of stress**, making it the most effective option when success is possible.

- Unassertive behaviour often leads to **suppressed resentment,** which later erupts as aggression and worsens stress.

- Assertiveness is **rational, constructive, and stress-relieving,** as misunderstandings are often unintentional and correctable.

- Speaking up respectfully can bring **positive changes** and significantly reduce emotional strain.

Key insight: Calm self-expression prevents resentment and restores balance.

2. Withdrawal – When Stress Becomes Overwhelming

- Withdrawal is useful when a situation **cannot be changed** through assertiveness or compromise.

- It may be **temporary** (to protect health and regain strength) or **permanent** (when no solution is possible).

- Temporary withdrawal can allow healing, reflection, and regrouping.

- Habitual or permanent withdrawal, if misused, may limit **growth and life satisfaction.**

Key insight: Withdrawal is helpful when used wisely—not as an escape from life.

3. Compromise – Staying Without Struggling

Compromise allows one to remain in a stressful situation with reduced conflict, especially when power is unequal or stalemates exist.

Common Forms of Compromise:

- **Conformity:** Adapting outwardly to changes when resistance causes more stress than acceptance.

- **Negotiation:** A healthier compromise involving **mutual adjustment** and shared solutions.

- **Substitution:** Achieving goals through **alternative means** when the original path is blocked.

Key insight: Compromise works best when the emotional cost is lower than the stress it prevents.

Final Reflection

- No strategy is inherently good or bad.

- The real measure is the **long-term impact on well-being.**

- Excessive compromise or passive adjustment may create **chronic stress.**

- A balanced life requires knowing **when to assert, when to step back, and when to adapt.**

Coping Strategies for Effective Management of Stress

Effective coping strategies for stress management are not one size fits all. Each person's response to stress can vary based on their unique situations and emotional triggers. It is essential to identify which coping strategies resonate with personal experiences.

Some Common Approaches Include

A. PROBLEM FOCUSED STRATEGIES

Derived from understanding stressors, they enable individuals to tackle challenges head-on through organized planning or seeking assistance Include developing time-management skills, avoiding procrastination and setting goals.

B. EMOTION FOCUSED STRATEGIES

Promotion of resilience by fostering emotional expression and acceptance, which are critical when facing unavoidable stressors involve the expression of emotion and often include the altering of expectations.

By applying these strategies to real- life situations people can better identify proper and appropriate coping mechanisms tailored to their specific resource improving their overall mental well being.

Lifestyle Changes and Building Resilience

There are lots of ways to cope with stressful situations To get the maximum benefit, try to incorporate these techniques into daily life and not just start when you begin to have symptoms of stress. Most people find relief using a combination of methods.

RELAXATION TECHNIQUES

- Calm your mind : Mindfulness meditation, massage and deep breathing exercises Pranayama can lower your heart rate and calm the mind. You can also listen to favorite tunes or to soothing sounds.

- Studies show that even laughing reduces the stress hormone cortisol and boosts mood. Watch a funny show or get together with someone who makes you .

PHYSICAL TECHNIQUES

- **Be physically active:** which releases endorphins and boosts resilience

- Exercise 30 minutes of moderate activity on a daily basis. Walking outside or exercising with friends can help boost moods. We can also try mindful physical exercises like yoga or Tai chi

- Eating a healthy diet reduces cravings and improves moods

- Aim for a more balanced diet rich in fresh fruits and vegetables, cut back on fatty foods caffeine and sugar.

- Improve your sleep habits by enhancing the mood and cognitive function.

- During the night 6 plus hours will be needed for sleep, turn off electronics create a soothing environment and unwind with a book or a warm bath to have better and deep sleep.

- Stop using substances like alcohol and quit smoking altogether.

COGNITIVE TECHNIQUES

Keep a diary or journal : Write down the days accomplishments, capture positive events of the day are three things for which you are grateful to the Universe.

Make "my time" which means try to do at least one thing a day that's just for you It could be mindfulness breathing meditation, getting together with a friend reading a book or working on a hobby.

Share your feelings : When you feel overwhelmed, connect with a trusted loved one or friend Hearing a voice can help either, in person or on the phone.

Take control : Use lists or smartphone apps to better manage your time and pare down to- do s. Try planning your day the evening before so you know what to expect and what you might need to postpone Give yourself permission 'to say no to other people's requests Adjusting habits, routines and priorities can also contribute to stress management.

Seeking professional Help : This may be useful especially if the stress is overwhelming ;seeking guidance from a therapist or a counsellor can help to surmount your stress

Management Techniques for Combating Stress

- Stress is a natural, adaptive response of the body meant for survival (eustress), preparing the individual for fight or flight.

- Stress becomes harmful (distress) only when the response is not resolved or discharged.

- Effective stress management, therefore, focuses not on eliminating stress, but on timely regulation, release, and restoration of balance.

Managing Physical Stress

Nature of Stress

- Caused by accidents, burns, surgeries, infections, and physical trauma.

- Places direct strain on the body's physiological systems.

Management Techniques

- Adequate rest and recovery

- Balanced nutrition and hydration

- Gentle physical activity (walking, yoga, stretching)

- Proper sleep hygiene

- Medical care combined with relaxation techniques to prevent prolonged stress reactions

Managing Psychological and Emotional Stress

Nature of Stress

- Arises from fear, anxiety, worry, anger, jealousy, emotional conflicts, and excitement.

- Can be acute or chronic, leaving deep subconscious impressions if unresolved.

Management Techniques

- Awareness and emotional recognition rather than suppression

- Mindfulness and meditation to calm mental fluctuations

- Breath regulation (slow, deep breathing) to stabilize the nervous system

- Cognitive restructuring—changing unrealistic expectations and negative thought patterns

- Healthy emotional expression through communication, writing, or counselling

Managing Stress in Modern Life

Nature of Stress

- High-speed living, constant stimulation, competition, and social expectations

- Emotional hypersensitivity and reduced tolerance to frustration

Management Techniques

- Clear goal-setting and prioritization

- Time management and realistic workload planning

- Periodic digital and sensory detox

- Cultivating equanimity and emotional maturity

- Developing interpersonal skills to reduce relational stress

Avoiding Maladaptive Coping

Problem

- Suppression of stress through drugs, alcohol, or emotional repression

- Temporary relief followed by deeper physiological and psychological imbalance

Healthy Alternatives

- Physical activity and relaxation practices

- Social support and meaningful connection

- Creative outlets (music, art, laughter)

- Reflective practices such as self-inquiry and introspection

Managing the Stress Problem

Forms of Stress—physical, emotional, or psychological—produce a common physiological stress reaction.

Stress management aims to:

- Interrupt this reaction early

- Restore homeostasis

- Prevent psychosomatic disorders

Core Tools

- Relaxation response

- Breath awareness

- Meditation

- Lifestyle balance

- Positive mental attitude

Underlying Instructions for Tackling Stress

- Stress is inevitable; suffering is optional.

- When stress is recognized, regulated, and released, it becomes a force for growth, rather than disease.

- True stress management lies in harmonizing body, mind, and emotions, not merely controlling external situations.

Symptoms of Stress on Body

Stress, especially when prolonged or unresolved, does not remain confined to the mind alone. It gradually manifests through the body, emotions, and behavior, sending clear warning signals that the individual is under strain. Recognizing these symptoms early is a crucial step in effective stress management.

Sleep Disturbance

One of the earliest and most common symptoms of stress is disturbed sleep. An overstimulated mind finds it difficult to relax, leading to difficulty in falling asleep, frequent awakenings, or unrefreshing sleep. Chronic stress keeps the nervous system in a constant state of alertness, preventing the deep restorative rest necessary for physical and mental renewal. Over time, poor sleep further aggravates stress, creating a vicious cycle of exhaustion and anxiety.

High Blood Pressure

Persistent stress activates the body's "fight or flight" response, releasing stress hormones such as cortisol and adrenaline. While this response is useful in short-term emergencies, prolonged activation places excessive strain on the cardiovascular system. Elevated blood pressure becomes a common outcome, increasing the risk of heart disease, stroke, and other lifestyle-related disorders. Stress-induced hypertension is often silent, making it especially dangerous if left unmanaged.

Loss of Appetite

Stress can significantly alter eating patterns. For some individuals, it suppresses appetite, leading to reduced food intake and nutritional deficiencies. Emotional tension diverts the body's energy away from digestion, as survival mechanisms take precedence. Prolonged loss of appetite can weaken immunity, reduce energy levels, and impair the body's natural healing processes.

Indigestion

The digestive system is highly sensitive to emotional states. Stress disrupts the normal functioning of the gut, leading to indigestion, acidity, bloating, or irregular bowel movements. When the mind is agitated, digestive secretions and gut motility are affected, impairing proper assimilation of nutrients. This "gut–mind" imbalance is a clear indicator that emotional stress is spilling over into physical health.

Inexplicable Muscle Pain/Fatigue

Chronic stress often leads to constant muscle tension, especially in the neck, shoulders, back, and jaw. Over time, this tension results in unexplained aches, stiffness, and persistent fatigue. Even without physical exertion, the body feels drained because stress keeps muscles in a semi-contracted state, reducing circulation and oxygen supply.

This fatigue is not relieved by rest alone, as its root cause lies in mental and emotional overload.

Low Productivity

Stress directly impacts cognitive functions such as concentration, memory, and decision-making. An overwhelmed mind struggles to focus, leading to reduced efficiency and frequent errors. Tasks that once felt manageable begin to feel burdensome, resulting in procrastination and frustration. Low productivity further increases stress, creating a downward spiral that affects both professional performance and self-confidence.

Effects of Stress on Personalities

Which Personality Are You ?

TYPE A		TYPE B	
(a)	Very Competitive	1.	Non-Competitive
(b)	Always in a Hurry	2.	Relaxed, in Control
(c)	Tough and Hard	3.	Easygoing
(d)	Demands Perfection	4.	Understanding
(e)	Ambitious, Wants Quick Promotion	5.	Confident and Happy
(f)	Workaholic	6.	Enjoys Leisure & Weekends

Type 'A' Personalities

Sense of Time Urgency :

They have 'hurry sickness' always trying to stuff more into less time. They crate deadlines if none exists and substitute the quick for the better .

'B' personalities find time to ponder, weigh alternatives, experiment; they feel there is plenty of time.

Quest for Numbers:

Numbers, rupees, dollars, of acheivements, or other quantifiable items, are indices of prowess and achievement to the Type 'A'.

'B' personalities are more quality than quantity oriented.

Insecurity of Status:

'A' are outwardly confident and self-assured, but are often insecure underneath. They are constsntly struggling for recognition through a number of acheivements. They do not measure themselves by present status, but by the rate at which it improves.

Aggression and Hostility :

'A' s are extremely competitive. They tend to always challenge other people-in sports, games, work, or even discussions. Their free-floating hostility is not easily detected, but there is often a note of rancour in their speech. They might fume at something a 'B' personality will pass right over or laugh at.

Extra – Organisational Stress

- Family Life Events

- Social/Technological Changes

- Economic/Financial Aspects

- Relocation

Operation of Stress

Levels at which Stress Operates

Emotional disturbances in the personalities who face one or more of the above life events not only decrease their efficiency after a certain period and cause health hazards but also cause worries that affect the quality of their lives.

Stress Reaction

What happens to the body due to stress reaction?

- Stored sugar and fats pour into the blood stream to provide fuel for quick energy.

- The breath rate shoots up,providing more oxygen.

- Red blood cells flood the blood-stream ,carrying more oxygen to the muscles of the limbs and the brain.

- The heart speeds up and blood pressure soars,enduring sufficient blood supply to needed areas.

- Blood-clotting mechanisms are activated to protect against injury,muscles get tense in preparation for strenuous action.

- Digestion slows down ,so that blood may be diverted to muscles and brain.

- Perspiration and saliva increase.

Functions of Autonomic Nervous System

Function of Internal Organ	Stimulation	
	Sympathetic	Parasympathetic
Heart		
A. Pulse Rate	Increases	Decreases
B. Blood Pressure	Increases	Decreases
Sweating	Increases	Decreases
Eyes		
A. Pupils	Dilates	Constricts
B. Eye Lids	Widely open	Relaxed drooping
Blood Glucose	Increases	Decreases

Psychological Reactions

Unlike the body's stress reactions, our psychological reactions are shaped by learning and are heavily dependent on the way we view or perceive the whole world. There are different varieties of cognitive, emotional , and behaviourial responses to stress. There is bound to be an uncomfortable and unpleasant feeling among victims of stress that something bad is about to happen –the most familiar psychological reactions to stress . These are referred to as defense mechanisms or 'ego mechanisms' since they are used to protect oneself from perceived threats. Each of us rely on such mechanisms when we feel threatened and are used to maintain our sense of self-worth or inadequacy.

Effective Management of Stress Through Lifestyle Changes

Effective stress management is not merely about reacting to pressure; it is about **designing one's life consciously**.

Individuals who manage stress well do so, because they cultivate clarity, purpose, balance, and healthy interpersonal habits.

The following traits are commonly found in people who remain calm, productive, and resilient even in demanding situations

Those who have Clear Life and Professional Goals

People with clearly defined life and professional goals experience less anxiety and confusion. Goals give direction to effort and meaning to struggle. When one knows *why* one is working, temporary pressures lose their power to overwhelm the mind. Clear goals act as anchors during turbulent times, helping individuals stay focused rather than emotionally reactive.

Goals that are Very Clear and Realistic

Unrealistic expectations are a major source of stress. Those who manage stress effectively set clear, achievable, and time-bound goals. They assess their strengths, limitations, and available resources honestly. Realistic planning prevents frustration, burnout, and the sense of constant failure, allowing steady progress with peace of mind.

Focus on Professional Growth

Stress reduces when individuals invest in **continuous learning and skill development**. Professional growth builds confidence and adaptability, making challenges feel manageable rather than threatening. People who update their skills and remain open to change are less fearful of competition, uncertainty, or technological shifts, thereby maintaining emotional balance at work.

Positive Mental Attitude

A positive mental attitude does not deny difficulties; it faces them with courage and optimism. Such individuals interpret challenges as opportunities to learn rather than as personal failures. This mindset reduces unnecessary worry, strengthens emotional resilience, and helps the mind remain calm under pressure.

High Degree of Enthusiasm

Enthusiasm is a powerful antidote to stress. When individuals are genuinely interested in their work, fatigue and pressure are felt less intensely. Enthusiasm fuels motivation, sustains energy, and brings joy into daily activities. A joyful mind is naturally more stress-resistant.

Very Clear-Cut Priorities

Stress often arises from trying to do everything at once. Effective stress managers understand what is urgent, important, and secondary. By prioritizing tasks wisely, they conserve mental energy and avoid last-minute panic. Clear priorities lead to better time management and a greater sense of control over life.

Good Human Relation Skills

Healthy relationships significantly reduce stress. Individuals who respect others, show empathy, and handle conflicts maturely create a supportive emotional environment. Good human relations at home and work reduce misunderstandings, resentment, and emotional exhaustion, fostering inner peace and cooperation.

Very Good Communication Skills

Clear and respectful communication prevents confusion, conflict, and emotional tension. People who express their thoughts calmly and listen attentively avoid unnecessary stress caused by assumptions or misinterpretations. Effective communication builds trust, reduces friction, and enhances teamwork.

Ability to Delegate Work

Trying to do everything alone is a sure path to stress. Effective stress managers understand the value of delegation. By assigning tasks according to others' strengths, they reduce overload and increase efficiency. Delegation also builds teamwork, mutual trust, and shared responsibility.

Simple Techniques for Resilience

The 5 r's of stress management are a framework for effectively dealing with stress, encompassing rethink, relax, release, reduce, and reorganize. This approach helps individuals to identify and manage stressors, promote relaxation, and build resilience.

Here's a breakdown of each R:

- **Rethink:**

This involves challenging negative or irrational thoughts and replacing them with more positive and realistic perspectives.

- **Relax:**

This focuses on activities that promote calmness and reduce tension, such as deep breathing, meditation, or spending time in nature.

- **Release:**

This involves finding healthy ways to express or let go of pent-up emotions, like exercise, creative expression, or talking to someone you trust.

- **Reduce:**

This entails identifying and minimizing stressors in your environment or lifestyle, such as overcommitting or unhealthy relationships.

- **Reorganize:**

This involves improving time management, prioritizing tasks, and creating a more balanced and manageable schedule.

Key Factors to Recognize Stress

- **Healthy Lifestyle:** Identifying personal stress triggers and understanding how stress manifests in your body and mind is crucial

- **Exercise:** Regular physical activity can improve mood and reduce anxiety.

- **Nutrition:** A balanced diet can support the body>s ability to cope with stress.

- **Sleep:** Prioritizing sufficient sleep is essential for both physical and mental recovery.

Relaxation Techniques:

- **Meditation and Mindfulness:** Practices like meditation and mindfulness can help calm the mind and reduce overthinking.

- **Deep Breathing Exercises:** Simple breathing techniques can be effective in managing immediate stress responses.

- **Progressive Muscle Relaxation:** This technique involves tensing and releasing different muscle groups to relieve physical tension.

Cognitive Strategies

- **Reframing:** Challenging negative thoughts and replacing them with more positive or realistic ones.

- **Setting Realistic Goals:** Avoiding perfectionism and setting achievable goals can reduce pressure and stress.

- **Time Management:** Organizing tasks and prioritizing effectively can help reduce feelings of being overwhelmed.

Seeking Support

- **Building a Support System:** Having friends, family, or support groups to talk to can provide emotional support during stressful times.

- **Professional Help:** If stress is persistent or overwhelming, seeking guidance from a therapist or counselor can be beneficial.

- **Work-Life Balance:** Finding a balance between work, personal life, and social activities is crucial for long-term stress management.

- **Social Support:** Spending time with loved ones, joining support groups, or seeking professional guidance.

By incorporating these techniques into daily life, individuals can develop effective stress management strategies and improve their overall well-being

Benefits of Stress Management

- Improved physical and mental health.

- Enhanced ability to cope with challenges.

- Better job performance and productivity.

- Improved relationships.

- Increased motivation and enthusiasm.

Key Takeaways

- Stress management is about maintaining stress within an optimal range, not eliminating it entirely.

- A combination of healthy lifestyle choices, relaxation techniques, and cognitive strategies can be highly effective in managing stress.

- Finding the specific techniques that work best for you is crucial for individual well-being.

- Seeking professional guidance (counselling, therapy) is important if you are struggling with severe or chronic stress.

Observe a Regular Routine Mindfully

Here are some easy ways to incorporate exercise into your daily schedule:

- Put on some music and dance around.

- Take your dog for a walk.

- Walk or cycle to the grocery store.

- Use the stairs at home or work rather than an elevator.

- Park your car in the farthest spot in the lot and walk the rest of the way.

- Pair up with an exercise partner and encourage each other as you work out.

- Play ping-pong or an activity-based video game with kids.

- Join kids in indoor games like carroms, scrabble, crossword etc.

Stress Symptom Check-List

Some of the problems which are stress-related are given below :

Please mark the frequency with which you have experienced each of these problems during the last two months.

Use the following symbols in responding to the check-list :

X – never had the problem

C – constant or nearly constant occurrence

F – frequently

O – occassionally

Tension headaches	Fatigue
Nausea	Colitis
Irritability	Back pain
Migraine headaches	Depression
Early morning wakening	Allergy problems
Loss of appetite	Arthiritis
Nervousness	Diarrhoea

Nightmares	Worrisome thoughts
Aching neck &shoulders	Common flu or cold
Asthma attack	Peptic ulcer
High Blood pressure	Heart palpitations
Stomach indigestion	Sexual problems
Dermatitis	Angry feelings
Alcohol consumption	Others

Role of Music as a Stress-Relieving Solution

Essential Attributes of Music

Introduction

Music Intelligence is your natural ability to use music and sound as self-reflecting, transformational tools to facilitate total health and well-being. The breath/energy realm provides a link between the denser material body and the more subtle realm of the mind. According to Sufi Master and Indian Veena Maestro Hazrat Inayat Khan, "The breath is the result of a current which runs not only through the body, but also through all the planes of man's existence ....the current of the whole of nature is the real breath.....It is the one breath and yet it is many breaths."

- Music is a manifestation of an inner sound, cosmic sound which exists inside each one of us.

- Music opens the doors to other dimensions and offers us access to the knowledge and wisdom contained there.

- Music speaks to our physical, mental, emotional and spiritual bodies and provides us a direct connection to spirit.

- We connect to our inner being when we listen to or play music.

- Music is a language that the spirit understands clearly.

- When we listen to or play music we leave the mundane world and access balance, peace, contentment and serenity.

- Music helps us use sound and silence usefully.

Movement is vibration; vibration is sound. Music, therefore, is not an external creation but a remembrance of the original rhythm of life. Music Intelligence is the soul's natural ability to recognize this rhythm and align itself with it—using sound as a doorway to awareness, healing, and inner transformation.

Through music, the seeker touches dimensions beyond logic and emotion. It awakens cosmic memory, reminding the soul of its journey through countless realms. In moments of deep listening or inspired singing, the sense of individuality dissolves, and the listener becomes the listening itself.

When one listens or plays music with awareness, the mind loosens its grip on the mundane. The heart softens. The breath becomes harmonious. Peace, balance, and serenity arise without effort. Music opens subtle pathways leading inward—to the spirit center, the silent sanctuary of being.

Sound and silence then reveal their sacred unity. As Nāda Yoga teaches, sound ultimately leads to silence, and silence reveals Truth. Music allows us to experience the spiritual physically and the physical spiritually—a divine alchemy where body, emotion, and consciousness move in harmony.

Even at the cellular level, music exerts its grace. It touches organs, emotions, and energy fields, restoring balance and vitality. By aligning us with the cosmic rhythm, music strengthens our life force and gently guides us toward wholeness.

Thus, Essential Music Intelligence is not an accomplishment—it is a remembrance. A remembrance that we are born of sound, sustained by breath, and destined to return to silence.

Musicologists, music legends and eminent spiritual icons like Louise Montello, renowned Spiritual Singer Saint Thyagaraja Swamy, the saint of South India, Hazrat Inayat Khan, Frank Fitzpatrick of SOUL VISION, etc. have referred to music as an elixir for the mind which enable man to use sound as self-reflecting, transformational tools to facilitate total health and well-being. It has been proved that music has the ability to change your mood, reframe negative thoughts, and ease stress.

Find out how to fill your life with music that reduces daily stress.

- Begin your daily routine with soft music.

- Practice singing with the background of music.

- Play any musical instrument and enjoy.

- Reprogram any mantra with light music.

- Dance slowly with light music.

- Play music when stuck in traffic jams.

- Play music while performing household work.

- Listen to music before reclining or sleep.

- Organise a sonic diet -meet with music.

- While in a park, enjoy nature and music together.

Stress Among Children

Children reflect the consciousness of their parents. When your children are causing problems, look at what needs adjusting in your own life. A leading counsellor states when asked how to bring discipline among problem-children, she says that it is important at the first instance to look at the parents and ascertain how they feel about themselves and what values and attitudes they are giving their children. Until we deal with our own consciousness and take care of unfinished business, all our attempts to "fix" a problem-child are only going to compound the situation. The parent has to ask himself or herself "What is this challenge revealing to me? How can I be more loving and offer that love and tenderheartedness to my kids?"

Basic Challenges For Children

In today's fast-paced world it can be quite stressful to deal with a child's tantrums especially when there is no one around to assist the parent, who is single. Young minds need a lot of understanding and tenderness together with love to enable them to deal with all kinds of stress.

    a.   From early childhood, children are conditioned to excel in exams and achieve good grades. Consequently, we have become a mark-conscious society, which not only puts tremendous pressure on young minds but also suppresses their curiosity and independence. Society must introspect on why we stress so much on the highest grades. Most children are afraid of failing exams. The pressure to perform creates fear. Such strong fears created at a young age make the mind highly strung, and any trigger can break it.

b. Also during young age, sexual hormones rage in the body. Those energies need to be properly channeled. If left unattended, they create havoc on the self-confidence of the child not to speak of utter loneliness too.

c. Where the child faces the situation of angry arguments amongst parents, the child is bound to suffer mentally and emotionally while he stagnates in loneliness, thus feeling poor self-worth.

d. Parents of many children who are in stressful situations assume that their outpouring of love or affection can be equalled by a generous offering of money, gifts or possessions, which is patently wrong.

e. Children who are not healthy suffer from fear of being suppressed, may be in school or on any play ground if they are weak and frail. The young and formative minds suffer in silence and often becoming easy targets of bullying and intimidating seniors. The pressure of exams on young minds also aggravate their stress. Parents have a great role to play in shaping the minds of such unfortunate children lest they are forced to commit suicide.

Measures to Tackle Stress Among Children

If the parents can create conditions for a child to feel loved, appreciated, nurtured and supported by them, then he will be able to slowly progress mentally, physically and intellectually. Thereby, the parents would have created an environment in which their children experience high self-esteem and are free to discover and express their God-given talents. Too often we want to manipulate, force or coerce them into doing and being what we think they ought to be doing.

- We must help our children believe in themselves and in their ability to live their highest vision.

- Our role is to love them unconditionally, to support and guide them and to help them realize how loveable and capable they are. (To do this, we must feel lovable, capable and worthy ourselves.)

- Children reflect the consciousness of their parents. When the children are causing problems, look at what needs adjusting in your own life. It may possibly be one of a mindset or attitude of the parent.

- One way to help children is to instill in them a desire and interest in reading. If children read a lot, it will be good for their mind and their development.

- We can create conditions that allow us to sublimate any loneliness and suicidal thoughts into something positive, for example, by having children engage in challenging physical and creative work.

- Parents should spend more time with their children and create curiosity among them by making them aware that there are other things in life than only passing exams, thus making them aware that there are other avenues of employment besides engineering and medicine.

- Creating an interesting environment in school that children would love-like music, fine arts, painting etc. and sports activities, so that they will not revert to social media or mobile phones.

- Parents can enable the development of empathy and compassion in them through counselling services or spiritual practices like mindfulness meditation, yoga etc.

Unlocking the Joy of Music to Children

"Music is the shorthand of emotion. Emotions which let themselves be described in words with such difficulty, are directly conveyed to man in music, and in that is its power and significance. "   —Leo tolstoy

Psychological research has revealed that children are responsive to music and that Music affects the body directly through cells and organs and indirectly through emotions—which in turn strengthens our life force.

- Music goes a long way to enable infants and toddlers to ward off fears, trauma, inferiority complex, etc. and thereby eliminate stress. Child-development professionals say that sound and silence reveal their sacred unity and effectively assist children.

- Even at the cellular level, music exerts its grace. It touches organs, emotions, and energy fields, restoring balance and vitality. By aligning children with the cosmic rhythm, music strengthens their life force and help to balance their emotions.

- Music should be in every child's life, every day and adults should promote interested listening.

- Teachers and care-givers should look at the children and smile as they listen music together, to show that they enjoy the music.

Kahlil Gibran, the well-known Lebanese mystic, has given an important message that is addressed to parents through his spiritual masterpiece — "THE PROPHET".

- You may give them (your children) your love but not your thoughts.

- You may house their bodies but not their souls.

- For their souls dwell in the house of tomorrow, which you cannot visit, not even in your dreams.

- You may strive to be like them, but seek not to make them like you.

- For life goes not backward, nor tarries with yesterday.

- You are the bows from which your children as living arrows are sent forth.

Measures to Tackle Stress Among Children

If the parents can create conditions for a child to feel loved, appreciated, nurtured and supported by them, then he will be able to slowly progress mentally, physically and intellectually. Thereby, the parents would have created an environment in which their children experience high self-esteem and are free to discover and express their God-given talents. Too often we want to manipulate, force or coerce them into doing and being what we think they ought to be doing.

- We must help our children believe in themselves and in their ability to live their highest vision.

- Our role is to love them unconditionally , to support and guide them and to help them realize how loveable and capable they are. (To do this, we must feel lovable, capable and worthy ourselves.)

- Children reflect the consciousness of their parents. When the children are causing problems, look at what needs adjusting in your own life. It may possibly be one of a mindset or attitude of the parent.

- One way to help children is to instill in them a desire and interest in reading. If children read a lot, it will be good for their mind and their development.

- We can create conditions that allow us to sublimate any loneliness and suicidal thoughts into something positive, for example, by having children engage in challenging physical and creative work .

- Parents should spend more time with their children and create curiosity among them by making them aware that there are other things in life than only passing exams, thus making them aware that there are other avenues of employment besides engineering and medicine.

- Creating an interesting environment in school that children would love — like music, fine arts, painting etc. and sports activities, so that they will not revert to social media or mobile phones

- Parents can enable the development of empathy and compassion in them through counselling services or spiritual practices like mindfulness meditation, yoga etc.

Section B

Spritualty for Stress Management

Spirituality in Our Daily Life

Spirituality is no longer confined to a day of worship or a sacred place. It is woven into the fabric of daily life:

- In the market at work or while cleaning the home we are still spiritual beings.

- Ceremonies bring beauty but they are no longer seen as the only way to connect to the Divine.

- Our spiritual path is not limited to the church or temple or synagogue or mosque ; It lives in how we love, how we give, and how we live.

A learned life coach has stated, "it is my firm belief that spirituality is not an abstract, complex pursuit that it is often made out to be. It is born out of an inner inspiration, an awakening to the realization that there is more to life than materialism." Gautham Buddha has stated "Verily, I say unto you, your mind is spiritual, but neither is the sense-perceived void of spirituality! The eternal verities which dominate the cosmic order are spiritual, and spirit develops through comprehension. Better than worshipping of gods is obedience to the laws of righteousness."

Spirituality does not mean turning your back on life: it is not renunciation or ascetism; it is not running away from the problems of life. It is the source of courage and inner strength that will enable you to take on life's challenges in the awareness that you are a spark of Divinity; that within you is a shakti (strength) that is of the Infinite!

Spirituality facilitates a deeper contemplation of the reality. With a mature understanding and realization of of reality through spiritual practices and its philosophical analysis, a student or any layman would have a better knowledge of the daily struggles of life including stressful situations and how these can be resolved easily. With spirituality, we create a world where we nourish humanity by creating a world free from fear and discrimination where every citizen feels safe—emotionally, mentally, and spiritually.

Why Spirituality is Indispensable for a Stress-Free-Living?

"Spirituality exists wherever we struggle with the issue of how our lives fit into the greater cosmic scheme of things. This is true even when our questions never give way to specific answers or give rise to specific practices such as prayer or meditation. We encounter spiritual issues every time we wonder where the universe comes from, why we are here, or what happens when we die. We also become spiritual when we become moved by values such as beauty, love or creativity that seem to reveal a meaning or power beyond our visible world. An idea or practice is 'spiritual' when it reveals our personal desire to establish a felt-relationship with the deepest meanings or powers governing life. ”

—Robert C. Fuller

Spiritual Well-Being

Well-being has something to do with order and with harmony. Order means everything has its right place, everything works together properly, each bit playing its part well in harmony with everything else. Similarly, we feel good in a group where many work together well, each one making his or her contribution toward everyone's well-being. Working together means primarily—mutual giving and taking according to the needs and the capacities of the various individuals.

When someone moves away from the right place, the order is disturbed and with it, the good feelings in the family only. When all the family members can feel good, does the individual also feel good. Beyond our physical well-being, we feel well in our SOUL. Here too, the well-being depends on order and harmony, on thoughts and feelings being in order. The spiritual well-being comes from harmony with spiritual forces and spiritual power. When there is harmony with spiritual power we can turn to everything as it is. We are connected to everything as it is, with love. NOTHING stands in the way of our well-being.

Perfect Happiness

What Is Happiness?

Happiness is something we all recognize when we experience it, even though it is difficult to define. It may appear as relief, harmony, peace and relaxation, or as enthusiasm, inspiration and quiet joy. While our understanding of happiness evolves with age and experience, its essence remains the same—**a sense of inner balance and well-being**.

Happiness is deeply **internal**. It is not something we acquire from the outside but a **gift we give ourselves**, rooted in the ***here and now***. As we mature, happiness becomes subtler—less a loud laugh and more a gentle smile that rises from within.

Happiness and Human Evolution

What makes us happy depends largely on our **stage of inner evolution** and **temperament**:

- **Physical happiness** — comfort, health, sensual pleasure.

- **Emotional happiness** — relationships, desires, excitement.

- **Intellectual happiness** — learning, understanding, clarity.

- **Spiritual happiness** — selflessness, love, wisdom, inner peace.

These correspond broadly to:

- **Tamasic tendency** — inertia and bodily comfort.

- **Rajasic tendency** — ambition, emotion and restlessness.

- **Sattvic tendency** — harmony, compassion and wisdom.

All these exist in every human being in varying proportions and may change over time. Hence, judging another's level of happiness or evolution is both difficult and unnecessary.

The Inner Nature of Happiness

A happy person is **not one without problems**, but one who has learnt to face life with maturity and balance. Happiness does not eliminate grief, but it gives us the strength to regain equilibrium. Life, like water, always seeks balance.

Comparing ourselves with others is one of the greatest causes of unhappiness. The only meaningful progress is **becoming better than our own past self**. Guilt and regret weaken happiness; sincerity to one's inner truth protects it.

True happiness arises when:

- We are **true to ourselves**

- We love and are loved

- We respect and are respected

- We trust and are trusted

- We feel connected—to ourselves, others, and life itself

The Three Spiritual Paths to Happiness—Human fulfillment unfolds through three complementary paths:

- **The Path of Action** – selfless service

- **The Path of Devotion** – pure love and surrender

- **The Path of Knowledge** – wisdom and understanding

Perfect happiness requires the **integration of all three. Perfect Happiness = Perfect Service + Perfect Love + Perfect Wisdom**

Qualities of Perfect (Spiritual) Happiness

Spiritual happiness is our natural state, though fully known only through experience. Even now, its principles can reduce **stress and suffering:**

- Happiness and sorrow are **complementary**, not enemies

- Both are **relative** and temporary

- Karma is not punishment, but a **teacher**

- There is deep joy in **doing what is right**, even when difficult

- Happiness naturally **radiates** and uplifts others

- Rejoicing in others' success purifies the heart

- **Equilibrium (inner balance)** is the essence of lasting happiness

- True happiness brings **serenity**, where **stress** cannot survive

Yoga, in essence, is this equilibrium—inner harmony reflected outwardly.

In Essence

Life does not promise constant bliss. Therefore, each individual must **discover and create moments of happiness** through awareness, right living, and spiritual alignment. As consciousness evolves, happiness becomes calmer, deeper, and more radiant. When happiness matures into serenity, **stress dissolves naturally**, and life flows in tune with its inner rhythm.

There is a story from the Hasidic Jewish Teachings which illustrates thus :

A certain man met a rabbi (a Jewish preacher) who was a sage. The rabbi asked him how he was. The poor man said " It is terrible. There are ten of us living in one room. " The rabbi said, "Take your two goats into the room with you." When the rabbi next met him and asked how he was, the poor man said, "Oh! It is unbearable, how with the goats also in the room. And the smell!" The rabbi said, "Now take the goats out of this room." When they met next, the poor man said, "It is wonderful now! Without the goats, we have plenty of space."

So, we can always be thankful that things are not worse! And however bad things maybe, we can always see people who are worse off than ourselves and whom we may be able to help. Let us think of them and not of ourselves. Perhaps in helping them we can forget our own unhappiness.

- There is no such thing as bad karma. There may be pleasant or painful karmic circumstances, but all karma is good karma, for karma is our teacher. In fact we learn more from a difficult fate than from easy circumstances.

- There is joy in doing what is right, even in the face of opposition and persecution. If we follow our conscience, even if it means difficulty, hardship and unhappiness , we experience joy at a deeper level.

- If we are happy, we spread happiness around us. This is something which we can ourselves experience. "If you are yourself full of happiness , that radiant joy is poured upon all who come near you, and you become a veritable sun," said C. W. Leadbeater, the popular theosophist.

- It is possible to rejoice in the happiness of others. Can we rejoice with someone who has succeeded where we have failed , who has achieved something which we wished to, but did not manage to

achieve? Rejoicing in others' happiness, is one
of the four *Brahma Viharas* or mental states to
cultivate a compassionate and loving heart as
advocated by Gauthama Buddha

- True happiness is a characteristic sign of progress,
  although then we do not think of progress. The
  more man progresses, the more radiant and joyful
  will be his consciousness. Stress of any kind will
  be non-existent when happiness leads to serenity
  which radiates from the face.

Towards Better Health — Soulful Living

1. Become conscious

Get to know your body's processes, and learn techniques such as mindfulness meditation, energy conservation etc.

2. Tap into your body's network

Own and release emotions that do not serve you. Do not take things personally. Develop Buddha's non-attachment in your daily life.

3. Honor your dreams

Some dreams are the psyche's way of bringing denied emotions to the surface so you can feel, deal and heal.

4. Know your body

The spine, skin and *Chakras* are your ports of entry into the body's conversations, so get massages, touch and hugs as often as you can. And find time for a brisk walk every day.

5. Reduce Stress

The fastest and easiest way to reduce stress is through meditation. Also focusing on your breathing releases many chemicals in the body which promote harmony.

Self-honesty, ie. being true to yourself, lowers stress in a big way. If you think of one thing, say another, do a third, and feel a fourth, your systems run at cross-purpoes. Far better is to declare your intent to yourself and then mobilize everything around that , the an engine leads the bogies and must pull in the same direction.

6. Regular exercise

A good brisk walk rleases lots of endorphins and gets the blood carrying oxygen and nutrients to all organs.

7. Eat wisely

The digestive system is a huge source of peptide messengers , so work with them. Eat only when you are hungry and stop when full. Do not eat when stressed, depressed or angry.... go for a walk instead. Avoid sugar. The body readily makes glucose, which fuels the brain, but ingesting sugar interferes with this natural process by flooding receptors in the liver. Food prepared from plants and vegetables infuse good energy into your body as there is no violence of any kind in their produce. Be a Vegetarian.

Anger—Manifestation of Stress

Anger as we all know is a common manifestation of stress, a vice prevalent in all of us to different degrees. Some are short-tempered but forget soon, some burn inside while others burst out. To different degrees, anger enslavens us. The more we get stuck with enslaving loop, the more we regret later —"Oh, how I wish I had not reacted in a hurry. I feel ashamed myself. ; A sense of guilt is not uncommon.

What is the cause of anger?

Things do not happen the way we want, people around us do not respond the way we expect them to, the boss or the employer hurts our ego, our prestige is at stake, even suspicion can trigger anger. While seeing some unjust, unlawful atrocious situation around us, we are provoked to anger and we react. Tolerance is propagated by the UNESCO as HARMONY IN DIFFERENCE. It is a virtue that makes peace possible within ourselves and outside. Tolerance is respect, acceptance and appreciation of the rich diversity of our world's cultures , forms of expression and ways of being human. WE MUST USE THE POWER OF TOLERANCE IN PLACE OF ANGER TO RISE SPIRITUALLY.

Gauthama Buddha showed humanity the important steps to eradicate sorrow, and tolerance is a major step. He advised "removal of negative thoughts, also called distracting, unwholesome, or evil thoughts connected with desire, hate, anger and delusion. Such thoughts are blameworthy and lead to suffering and misery. Think about the negative consequences they bring (stress, regret, bad karma, harm to self or others".

(Extracted from Vitakkasanthana Sutta)

Seven Drawbacks Of Anger (from Buddhist Wisdom)

Taken from the *Kodhana Sutta* (**Sutta** refers to doctrines or precepts)also known as "The Wretchedness of Anger')

The sutta describes seven things that are pleasing to an enemy (i. e. they help fulfil an enemy's wishes) and happen to a person overcome by anger (krodha). The Buddha explains how anger harms the angry person themselves, making them ugly, sleepless, confused about gains/losses, destructive, isolated and ultimately leading to rebirth in a bad destination.

Considered as the seven drawbacks :

1. An angry person becomes ugly—even if well groomed and dressed nicely, anger makes them look repulsive (an enemy doesn't like seeing their foe look good).

2. An angry person sleeps poorly—anger causes restlessness and bad sleep (an enemy wishes their foe to sleep badly).

3. An angry person misjudges profit or loss and when they suffer a loss they think it is a gain. When they gain something they think it is a loss This confusion turns real benefits into harm.

4. An angry person loses property or wealth and anger leads to actions that destroy or squander what they have.

5. An angry person loses friends and reputation. People avoid them and their good name is ruined.

6. An angry person loses his sense of shame and conscience. He acts without moral restraint.

7. An angry person is reborn in a bad destination (like hell)-Ultimately anger leads to suffering in future lives.

The *sutha* ends with verses emphasizing that anger blinds a person to the *Dhamma*, **(righteousness)** wraps them in darkness, and causes lasting harm

The antidote is to abandon anger through taming the mind and that will lead to freedom from defilements.

Emotional Quotient

EMOTION QUOTIENT OR EQ is a positive and proactive attitude towards all aspects of life or the ability to get along with people and situations.

There are four Basic Components to evaluate emotional intelligence. They are as follows:

a. Understanding one's own emotions and motivating oneself.

b. Proactively empathizing with others.

c. Building a conducive environment to achieve higher team goals.

d. Coping with the changing circumstances.

How to Bring Intelligence to Emotion?

While IQ is a genetic that cannot be changed by life experiences, it is a moot question as to what factors are at play when people of high IQ flounder while those with modest IQ do surprisingly well.

The difference quite often lies in abilities called emotional intelligence. This includes self control, zeal, persistence and the ability to motivate oneself. Importance of EQ is valuable in the fabric of society when selfishness, violence and a meanness of spirit seem to be rotting the goodness of our communal life. The argument for the importance of emotional intelligence hinges on the link between sentiment, character and moral instincts. The ability to control impulse is the base of will and character. Those who are at the mercy of Impulse (which is the medium of emotion), lack self control and suffer a moral deficiency. The root of altruism and compassion lies in empathy, the ability to read emotions in others; lacking a sense of another's need or despair—there is no caring.

Developing Emotional Intelligence

SIGNS OF HIGH EMOTIONAL INTELLIGENCE

If your emotional quotient or intelligence is reasonably high, it necessarily means that you have the following qualities:

- You're honest and transparent

- You're open minded and receptive to new ideas

- You articulate your points clearly

- You stay under pressure

- You're a good listener

- People feel relaxed working with you

- You provide feedback effectively

- You understand other's perspectives

- You're self-motivated

- You create and maintain networks

- You effectively manage stress and setbacks
- You handle criticism constructively
- You can share your worries and concerns
- You can settle disputes and misunderstandings
- You provide a vision that motivates others.

Training the Mind (Through Meditation and Mindfulness)

In seeking a meaningful life rooted in love and wisdom, devoid of stresses and strains of our daily lives, few guides are more helpful than the training of the mind. Among the most revered in Tibetan tradition is the *EIGHT VERSES FOR TRAINING THE MIND* composed by the 11th century Tibetan Master Langri Tampa.

These verses are practical teachings that show us how to transform daily life into a path of compassion and insight so that man lives his life free of tension and stress.

1. First Verse Sets the Foundation

By thinking of all sentient beings as more precious than a wish-fulfilling jewel, for accomplishing the highest aim, I will always hold them dear. Through them we learn patience, kindness, and humility.

2. Second Verse Encourages Humility

Whenever I am with others, I will see myself as the lowest among all, from the depths of my heart, I will hold others as supreme. By lowering our sense of self-importance, we open ourselves to genuine connection and compassion

3. Third Verse Turns the Mirror Inward

In all my actions, I will examine my mind. The moment a disturbing emotion arises, I will confront and avert it firmly. Training the mind requires vigilance. Anger, jealousy and pride may arise—but by observing them without judgement, we learn not to be controlled by them.

4. Fourth Verse Asks us to View Difficult People as Treasures

Whenever I meet a person of bad nature, overwhelmed by negativity and suffering, I will cherish them as rare treasure. It is easy to love those who are kind to us. But the true test of compassion lies in our response to those who test our patience. Their suffering is often hidden behind anger. To meet them with compassion is to live *Dharm,* i.e. adopting Righteousness.

5. Fifth Verse Offers a Radical Response to Harm

When others, out of envy, treat me wrongly with abuse and scorn, I will accept defeat amd offer the victory to them. This is not passivity. It is the strength to let go of ego. When we abandon the need to win or be praised, we create space for peace.

6. Sixth Verse Addresses Betrayal

When someone I have helped , deeply hurts me, I will regard them as my supreme teacher. Betrayal is painful, but it also reveals our attachments and expectations. If we can learn rather than close our hearts , we grow in resilience and understanding.

7. Seventh Verse Expresses the Heart of *Bodhicitta*

In short, both directly and indirectly, I will offer help and happiness to all, and secretly take upon myself their suffering. This verse points to the practice of taking in other's pain and sending out joy.

8. Eighth and Final Verse Turns to Wisdom

May I see all things as illusions, and, without attachment, gain freedom from bondage. The world appears solid and fixed, but in truth, all things are impermanent and interdependent. Understanding this frees us from grasping and allows us to act with compassion and clarity.

Together these verses offer a complete training—from cultivation of compassion to the realisation of wisdom and ensures mental calm and stability. They do not ask us to withdraw from life but to engage it with an open heart. Every challenge becomes a step on the path. Every person is a potential teacher. These verses remind everyone that the true work of the spiritual path is to transform the mind— from confusion to clarity, selfishness to love, agression to peace.

Surrender—Joy of Surrender

'Letting go, can empower your life!'

What is surrender?

Surrender does not mean that we give up every effort, leave all to some God or Almighty, to whom we are supposed to have surrendered and stay put. That is self-deception.

Surrender means ceasing to exercise our personal choice, personal preference, and submitting our will to the higher Will. It does not mean that we surrender our individuality. As a matter of fact by linking our will to a higher and more powerful Will, we enhance our effectivity; our individuality gets a content of higher light and force. If you have conscientious objections to surrender to someone outside yourself, even if it be God, then surrender to your own Higer Self. Thereby, we shift our allegiance from the lower nature to the higher: that is SURRENDER.

1. Why Does Life Become Easiest When You are Able to Let Go?

Surrender is the secret key to success, spiritual evolvement and health. When you are able to let go, you are able to follow more with the guidance of life and intuition and any messages you might be getting about life and how to lead it;instead of pushing , forcing and overthinking things. **(Surrender is when you go ahead with something that your guidance tells you to do and you are carried by the flow.)**

2. Why is it Important to "Get Out of Your Head" before You can Evolve into Surrender?

Surrendering means balancing your intellect with your intuition. When you get out of your own way and are able to sense (as well as think and intuit) you can experience an amazing balance. When you balance the head and heart, you get right into the flow of whatever you want ...success, intimacy, spiritual development, health ...you name it. (Example — determining who is your soul mate))

3. Can we Assume that Surrender is Not "Giving In" And how Spirituality Plays into Surrender?

Generally people think that surrender won't work , because they think it means failure or weakness, or giving in. But when you redefine it as something much larger than that, then you are surrendering to a Power much greater than yourself that can help you to gain more personal power and satisfaction; even ecstacy.

'Fear of death and the afterlife ' affects your ability to surrender on every level. When you can make peace with that and have a belief that you are not really surrendering yourself, you are becoming larger, you are becoming more, and there is nothing to be afraid of.........then it allows you to live your life more completely and more joyously now, without having that fear lurking underneath the surface.

4. It is Believed that We have a Biologically Determined Set Point for Happiness. If this is True, How can We Be Happier and Experience More Joy ?

You can change your happiness set point.... that is the miracle. Surrender is the way to do that. By surrendering to what is positive, surrendering to a meditation practice practice, surrendering stress and negativity, that can reset your happiness set point in ways that nothing external can.

For example somebody wins a lottery. Their happiness is short-lived and not enduring and it does not change the happiness set point. The only way to change it, is what has been said before i. e. meditate using 3 minutes to center yourself and then return to life. This will transform everything. (the 3 minute surrendering stress meditation)

5. Men and Women have Different Energies. Men are More Goal-Oriented and Fix-it Oriented. What is the Difference in their Mode of Surrender?

We each have a male and female inside of us, but women have a larger white matter tract that joins the right and left parts of the brain called the *corpus callosum,* so they are more able to integrate both emotional and mental activities: whereas men don't have that connection as much. As a result, men usually don't do more than one thing at a time very well. They often get overwhelmed if a woman is going on, from one thing to another to another. It's easier for a man to process one thing at a time.

Women need to know that, and not just go from one thing to another to another, and stay very focused with men. That helps the man to feel that he can help. Men love to be of service. They love to help, and they respond negatively if they feel like, nothing they do is enough.

6. How can Surrendering Fear Transform Our Money Situations ?

If you have a fear-based attitude toward money, it will constrict the flow of abundance. So, it's really important that you deal with your fears about money wherever they came from, say parents, early upbringing, or a spouse, etc. so that you can surrender to the flow of abundance. Abundance is a flow; it's an energy that you really need to attune to. Fear will stop that flow.

7. How can Surrender Expand Our Joy?

It is important to surrender to the joy of surrender and really absorb and savor it more each day. It sometimes is odd how we resist pleasure and joy. We see this with many of our close ones and sometimes we also resist it. The fear and the difficulties are somehow easier to absorb and focus than the joy.

Powerful Mantra for Blissful Living

Surrender to the joy every day, to the joy of being in the moment, and the joy of little things.

Every day, wake up,
Open your eyes and surrender.
Breathe and surrender.
As you are drinking your coffee, surrender !
...looking at the Universe, the sky,
...walking in nature, surrender and
revel in all of these things.

Don't take anything for granted, because life could be taken away in an instant, or it could be after some time.

So, embrace the bliss and ecstasy of SURRENDER and the joy of it as much as you can , every day.

Meditation is a Healthier Way to Cope With Stress

Meditation is a systematic, introspective practice to facilitate growth in three areas

- Getting to know the mind

- Training the mind

- Freeing the mind.

These three aspects of meditation are not unrelated or separate, but rather constitute a single process of inner exploration, discovery , and development that can be called the Meditative Way.

One of the main benefits of meditation is its ability to reduce stress. The body's stress response causes the body to automatically react in ways that prepare you to fight or run. In some cases of extreme danger, this physical response is helpful. However a prolonged state of such agitation can cause physical damage to every part of the body.

Meditation affects the body in exactly the opposite way that stress does—by triggering the body's relaxation response. It restores the body to a calm state helping the body repair itself and preventing new damage from the physical effects of stress.

Advantage of Meditation Over Other Methods to Combat Stress

- People with physical limitations may find it easier to practice than strenuous physical exercise for stress relief. Moreover no special equipment is required.

- Unlike enlisting the help of a professional to help you overcome stress, meditation is free and here you address yourself.

- Unlike some medications and herbal therapies meditation has no potential side effects.

- Meditation is always available and can be done anywhere at any time.

- It is amazingly effective in short term stress reduction and long-term health. The benefits of meditation can be felt in just one session of meditation

- Meditation helps with effective stress management; A healthier approach to coping with stress through meditation involves focusing your attention and quietening your mind which helps eliminate thoughts.

Benefits of Meditation

a. Promotes relaxation and reduces stress hormones.

b. It activates the body's relaxation response counteracting the effects of stress.

c.   It can lower the production of cortisol, the stress hormone and reduce blood pressure and heart rate.

d.   This physiological relaxation helps the body repair itself and prevent further damage from stress.

e.   It improves focus and reduces mental clutter. Meditation helps you focus your attention and quiet the stream of racing thoughts that can contribute to stress. It fosters a sense of peace and emotional balance by reducing mental clutter. Thereby, meditation can improve concentration and clarity making it easier to handle any stressful situation.

f.   It enhances emotional resilience and well being Regular meditation practice can increase emotional resilience allowing you to respond to stress more calmly It can also improve overall emotional well being and reduce symptoms of anxiety and depression.

g.   It cultivates a sense of calm and presence, helping you to connect with the current moment instead of dwelling on worries about the future or regretting about the past.

h.   Meditation can reduce anxiety and improve your ability to cope with stress, and promotes self-awareness.

i.   Meditation helps you become more aware of your thoughts emotions and physical sensations promoting self-understanding.

j. With increased self-awareness, you can help yourself identify and manage stress triggers more effectively Meditation is accessible to everyone It can be practiced anywhere making it a versatile tool for stress relief.

k. Combining meditation with yoga or deep breathing maximizes stress management in a sense meditation offers a powerful tool for managing stress by promoting relaxation reducing stress hormones improving focus and enhancing emotional well being.

Meditation involves cultivating three qualities essential to well-being: awareness, concentration, and serenity. AWARENESS may also be called MINDFULNESS and is the state of the "mind being fully present." An aware mind is not just conscious in the ordinary sense, because we can be conscious without being fully aware, without clearly knowing what we are doing, why we are doing it, and what we are feeling. In meditation, we want to cultivate that fullness of mind that lets us be truly sensitive to the present moment. Mindfulness makes this type of introspection and exploration possible. It is an essential element in the practice of meditation, and only through the development of this quality of mindfulness can we cultivate concentration and serenity.

Mindfulness Meditation

Mindfulness with Breathing is a meditation technique anchored in our breathing. It is an exquisite tool for exploring life through subtle awareness and active investigation of the breathing and life. Before one starts with their meditation, it is very important to build a strong foundation of morality (*sila*). The precepts advised by Buddha are essential to the development and purity of mind. They provide the mind with general mindfulness and awareness which helps one to have a peaceful mind that is clear from any remorse or wrong doing. Mindfulness for Daily Life practice packs the essence of contemplative practices within your everyday routine. Based on scientific research that endorses its various benefits, Mindfulness is the most suited practice to accompany the modern day pace of life. It is not another meditation technique but a cultivation of the quality of meditative mind all the time.

Annexure

How To Do Meditation?

RIGHT POSTURE

Sit comfortably—either on the floor, (or) on the chair, (or) on the sofa.

Clasp your hands, cross your feet.

If you are wearing glasses (spectacles), remove them, and gently close your eyes

OBSERVATION OF THE BREATH

Witness your simple, easy, tender, normal, Natural Breath.

When you're with your breath, your mind naturally becomes empty.

Whenever thoughts arise, immediately bring your attention back to your NATURAL BREATH.

COMPLETION OF MEDITATION

Unclasp your hands and place your fingers on your eyes for five seconds Gently open your eyes by slowly removing your fingers.

Benefits of Meditation

Benefits of Meditation are manifold :

- Mind naturally stays in **Peaceful** and **Joyful** state

- **Memory** power increases

- Wasteful **Habits** die naturally

- Diseases gets **Healed** faster

- **Efficiency** in all work increases

- Heightened **Awareness**

- Ability to **Discern** right and wrong gets sharpened

- **Willpower** and **Self-Esteem** naturally become stronger

- Interpersonal **Relationships** become qualitative and fulfilling

- **Purpose of Life** is thoroughly understood

- Life becomes **Celebration**

and, many more...

SOULFULL FEDERATION TRUST ®

Lord Buddha's clarion call to 'be a light unto oneself' encouraged him to set up an institution i.e., a Charitable Trust named SOULFULL FEDERATION TRUST® in the year 2018 to spiritualise and enlighten individuals about meditation, holistic living, etc. free of cost. More than 10,000 meditation sessions under the auspices of the trust have been conducted so far while the activity to publish and circulate spiritual wisdom has just taken roots. It is our earnest appeal to all spiritual seekers to support the mission of the trust by their donation.

Dhyāna Ratna S.K. Rajan
Chairman
Soulfull Federation Trust®

SOULFULL FEDERATION TRUST®
.....springboard for enlightenment

BANK ACCOUNT :
  SOULFULL FEDERATION TRUST
  A/C NO.6357101001 1399
  CANARA BANK
  IFSC-CNRB 0016494
GOOGLE PAY -PHONE PE -PAY TM

Please scan and donate to support our mission.

About the Author —
Dhyāna Ratna S. K. Rajan

Dhyāna Ratna S. K. Rajan is a retired senior banker whose life took a profound spiritual turn after a series of transformative encounters with illumined souls and realised masters. These blessed interactions opened before him the deeper dimensions of life and awakened an inner call to tread the path of Dhyāna and Self-discovery. A seeker by temperament and a voracious reader by habit, he found his true joy in imbibing the timeless teachings of great sages and spiritual luminaries who have guided humanity across the ages.

At the gentle urging of revered spiritual mentors, he took to writing—so that the distilled wisdom of the Masters could be shared with earnest seekers every where. His works span a wide range of spiritual and self-elevating themes, drawing from the perennial teachings of Ādi Śaṅkarācārya, Gautama Buddha, Swami Sivanda and many other enlightened beings, as well as from insights on holistic living—encompassing physical, emotional, and mental purity. Through his writings, he aspires to rekindle in the reader a living spirituality—one that is not confined to ritual or tradition alone, but blossoms as a direct, heartfelt experience of the divine within.